The Jungle

SPIRITUAL DANGER AREAS
IN THE WORLD OF WORK

The Jungle

Spiritual Danger Areas in the World of Work

Dr. Jim Croushorn

Guardian BOOKS

Belleville, Ontario, Canada

The Jungle

Copyright © 2002, Jim Croushorn

ISBN: 1-55306-308-2

First Printing: December 2001
Second Printing: April 2002

**For more information or
to order additional copies, please contact:**

www.spiritualjungle.com

Essence Publishing is a Christian Book Publisher dedicated to furthering
the work of Christ through the written word. *Guardian Books* is an
imprint of *Essence Publishing.* For more information, contact:
44 Moira Street West, Belleville, Ontario, Canada K8P 1S3.
Phone: 1-800-238-6376. Fax: (613) 962-3055.
E-mail: info@essencegroup.com
Internet: www.essencegroup.com

Printed in Canada
by

TABLE OF CONTENTS

Acknowledgements

I WANT TO THANK the following people for their time and insights: Bill Alfred, Dr. Dwight Anderson, Jim Barger, Dr. Ken Boutwell, Fran Buhler, Jim Eikeland, Shirley Eikeland, Virgina Glass, Larry Gonzales, Amalia Kane-Crawford, Dr. Senyoni Musingo, Jack Nix, Howard Rhodes, Dr. Gene Sherron, Ellen Williams, Mark Wodka and Doug Woodlief. Much of the content of the discussion of the danger areas came from interviews with these people.

I want to thank Fran Buhler particularly for his encouragement through the years. In 1979, shortly after coming to Tallahassee, my wife Linda and I were involved in a head-on automobile crash with Fran and Nancy Buhler. Fran, Nancy, and Linda were all hospitalized. Fran and Nancy had been in Tallahassee for a number of years and were much loved by many people. When folks came to visit them in the hospital, they also came by to see Linda. Due to this, we became integrated into the community and the First Baptist Church of Tallahassee very quickly. There have to be better ways of forming fast friendships and becoming integrated into a community and church than being in a head-on automobile crash, but since then Fran has been a special friend. He has written suggestions and tolerated numerous one sided discussions of this book. Thank you, Fran!

I am indebted to my talented son, Dr. John Croushorn, for the design and production of the front and back covers. These came at a time when I needed inspiration to push on to produce the book. After receiving the covers, I called him and told him that I was going to have to write something special to merit the covers. I have no idea who said "you can't tell a book by its cover." I trust that is not true, because I hope this book is as good as the covers. Thank you, John, for the covers and for your feedback and contributions regarding what has gone between them.

I appreciate the interest and support of my daughter, Amy Lynn. She shared the book with her friends in Atlanta, and that resulted in some important feedback.

My gratitude to my wife, Linda, cannot be measured. She has always been supportive of my projects, even if they were not projects she would have chosen. Those differences in perspective have added richness to our relationship.

INTRODUCTION

THE CHATTER OF A machine gun was the first announcement to Lt. Joe Green[1] that his platoon had been ambushed as they walked down a jungle trail in Vietnam. As I read the account of Joe's death in S.L.A. Marshall's, "Battles in the Monsoons,"[2] I kept asking myself what was he doing on a trail, an obvious danger area in hostile jungles.

That first burst of fire from the enemy mortally wounded Lt. Green, and killed his radio operator. Subsequent fire hit him a second time. Lt. Green turned his command over to a subordinate.

Although it has been over 30 years since I read that passage, I will be forever haunted by the author's closing statement. "Then Lt. Green died and it began to rain."

I knew Joe had been killed, as had a number of our classmates. (Note: two classmates received the Medal of Honor posthumously, Bob Hibbs and George Sisler. See their citations at www.army.mil/cmh-pg/mohviet.htm.)

I graduated from Infantry Officer Candidate School

(OCS) on June 22, 1965. That was the last OCS class to graduate before the 1965 build up of American troops in Vietnam. About thirty of us had signed up for Ranger and Airborne School before reporting to our units. I remember Joe Green particularly because he had asked me to sing at his wedding the day we graduated from OCS at Fort Benning.

We reported to the U.S. Army Ranger School at Ft. Benning, Georgia, on July 8, 1965.[3] Our class members had been assigned to Army units around the world. At the time we graduated from OCS, the only American soldiers in Vietnam were Special Forces and some Marines, which had been committed in March of *1965*. This changed dramatically with the large commitment of American forces that summer.

The build up of American forces was fast and furious. I remember at the time we graduated from OCS there was one student battalion at the Ft. Benning Infantry School with six companies. A year later there were six student battalions, each with six companies.

The Second Infantry Division was in support of the Infantry School at Ft. Benning. Our OCS company commander had announced during the spring that six officers from each graduating class would go to the Second Infantry Division. Preference would be given to married men who wanted to stay in Columbus. Six of my married classmates requested assignment to the Second Infantry Division. I was assigned to the 1st Cavalry in Korea. Then a month after we graduated, the Second Infantry Division at Ft. Benning swapped colors with the 1st Cavalry in Korea. All those troops at Ft. Benning, including the six married volunteers out of our class, became a part of the 1st Cavalry Air Mobile. They were in Vietnam by the end of August.

When we all gathered at the Ranger School to sign in

on that very hot July afternoon, about half of the class members, including Joe Green, were told that their orders had been changed. They were told to report to their units immediately.

Each time I've thought of Joe's death, I've wondered if he had been allowed to go through Ranger School, would he ever have been on that jungle trail entrapped in an ambush.

THE REASON FOR THIS BOOK

Becoming a Christian is hard to understand but easy to do. Being a Christian is easy to understand but hard to do! This book is about the latter. Since you are reading this book, the assumption is that you are a Christian, and like the rest of us Christians can use all the help you can get in being a Christian day in and day out.

Most of us spend a majority of our waking hours at work earning a living. Because of the amount of contact with other people there, and the many decisions each person makes about work tasks, there is no other segment of our lives where our values and philosophy of life are revealed more clearly and tested more rigorously. For Christians, this is where living their faith or failure to live their faith is most observable.

For most of my adult life I have worked for state governments, churches, the military, or universities. On several occasions over the past 36 years I've tried to write a book about the Christian in the world of work. But my efforts basically came to the conclusion that to live a successful Christian life in the world of work you simply needed to just go and be a good Christian. That never seemed to be enough guidance for the many Christians I've known and observed at work who continually failed as Christians in the workplace. Often they found themselves ensnarled in doing things that in retrospect were not consistent with their claim to be a Christian. They often seemed to have been surprised by their entanglement.

Some Christians state that knowing what they should do in a given situation is a very simple matter. They just ask, "What would Jesus do?" I don't think that works very well for most of us. It is too little too late! Continuing with my military analogy, that would be like a soldier asking in a combat situation, what would General Patton do, or a jungle fighter asking what would Che Guevara do? It assumes that you know that person so well that you know what he would do in a situation in which he may never have been. It also assumes that the individual thinks well on his feet, will be able to recognize the real situation, and will come up with the ideal solution and act on it in a very short time.

As you will see, the apostle Paul tells us spiritual warfare is much more complex. At the same time many of the spiritual danger areas that are found in the workplace are as common to most of us as a road or trail in a jungle. For those danger areas which we can identify with the help of those who have "been there and done that," we do not have to wait until we face a danger area to decide what we are going to do.

I've also found that doing what is right, even when it involves actions, which goes against management or the power base of the organization, seldom has the dire consequences I've been warned of by my colleagues.

In numerous discussions with my friend and minister, Fran Buhler, I eventually made the connection that the world of work is like a jungle, having many analogies to a real jungle. There are swamps, "wait-a-minute" vines, trees with a canopy that makes the jungle floor almost dark at mid-day, and all of the creatures found in a jungle that I was taught about in the U.S. Army Ranger School.

One of my areas of concentration in my graduate school days was General Systems Theory. General Systems Theory is the study and application of processes in one system that can be applied to help understand the working of a completely different system. In some sense General Systems Theory is the use of analogies from one system to another. I should have more quickly connected my Ranger School training on the jungles of Vietnam to the jungle of the world of work that Christians face daily, but it was slow to come. However, once it did, the analogies came fast and clear. The workplace is a dynamic and ever changing environment: a jungle. I've come to believe that understanding the many elements of that jungle can help a Christian live his or her faith more successfully.

WHAT THIS BOOK IS NOT

This book is **not** about evangelism. Evangelism is about enlisting new troops, recruiting new soldiers into God's spiritual army.

This book is **not** about discipleship. Discipleship is about training new troops. It's about making them better soldiers, teaching basic skills for recruiting more new troops.

This book is **not** about ethics or ethical behavior. There are many non-Christians who are ethical. Being ethical is not dependent on a person's relationship with God, although people who have real relationships with God will be ethical. Ethical behavior will be a by-product of the Christian following these procedures.

This book is **not** about missions. The overall mission of every Christian is to be in God's will and evangelize the world. As a Christian, you must determine what is God's will for your life and what is your God given mission.

This book is **not** intended to help you understand or enrich your relationship with God. The underlying assumption of this book is that you already have that. As a Christian, you have a personal relationship with Christ that is real. You have the Holy Spirit living in you as a result of your conversion to Christianity. You do everything you can to keep attuned to the presence of the Holy Sprit in your life.

This book **is** about events, people, and thoughts that can critically wound and damage your relationship with God.

This book **is** about what is out there in the world of work that can threaten your relationship with God. It is about recognizing situations that make that relationship vulnerable to the forces of evil. This book will help you protect that relationship.

This book **is** about developing procedures before you need them for dealing with spiritual challenges. This book is about the need to know and practice these procedures. Does it seem a little strange to think about consciously developing and practicing procedures for dealing with sin? Think of how many events we plan and rehearse for, such as speeches and presentations, athletic contest, etc. The positive impact of such planning and practicing are obvious. Why not do this for spiritual challenges?

This book focuses on the spiritual jungle we know as

the workplace. I want to help you better understand that jungle. I want you to know how to read the jungle, and not only survive your journey through that jungle, but live successfully and victoriously as you travel through that jungle.

This book has a modest goal of teaching you how to recognize some of the dangerous places in the workplace jungle, places where you are likely to be ambushed by "the forces of evil." In Ranger School these were called "danger areas." In this book they will be called "spiritual" danger areas.

Through the years, the U.S. Army Ranger School has developed many tools for the jungle fighter to help him recognize and deal successfully with danger areas. This book attempts to do the same for the Christian in the world of work. It is an attempt to develop tools that will help the Christian identify spiritual danger areas, learn protocols for dealing with spiritual danger areas when they cannot be avoided, and know immediate actions that can be taken when the Christian finds himself caught in a spiritual ambush.

THREE STANDARDS FOR THE READER

Before you are sent to the jungle, the Army's Ranger School conditions both your body and mind. They teach and reteach you how to be a good soldier. The assumption is that before you are committed to combat in the jungle you are going to be a good soldier. You will be ready and able to appropriately respond to whatever you encounter in the jungle.

It is critical to your understanding of what this book has to offer that the same can be said of your spiritual readiness. Reading further is a waste of your time unless you meet three standards:

- You are a Christian;
- You have no doubts that you are a Christian; and
- You are seriously trying to live a Christian life.

Without meeting these standards your time is wasted because this presentation assumes that the reader is a confident Christian who is serious about living a Christ-like life. If this is not true for you, the tools for successfully dealing with spiritual danger areas in the workplace will be hard to use.

So, if you are not a Christian, please go to Appendix A and deal with that issue before reading further. Then return to the next paragraph.

Note: The Non-Christian Reader reads Appendix A.

X OK. You are a Christian—either as a result of experiencing Christ as recommended in Appendix A, or because of an earlier experience.

Next: If you are a Christian but you have had doubts about whether your conversion experience was real, or have doubts that you really do have a personal relationship with God, go to Appendix B. Then remove all doubt about the reality of your relationship with God once and for all time before you read further. Serious jungle fighters do not have doubts about their relationship with their Commander and Chief.

Note: The Doubtful Christian Reader reads Appendix B.

Y OK. So now you are a Christian, and you have no doubts whatsoever that you have a real personal relationship with God. But you don't always try to live that relationship in your daily life. You still have a problem.

These tools for dealing with spiritual danger areas are not for the faint hearted or the Christian who is "playing" with religion like a hobby. These tools are for the serious jungle fighter. If you are not a serious spiritual jungle fighter, go to Appendix C and see what is involved in becoming one.

Note: The Confident Christian Reader who is only playing with his religion reads Appendix C.

Z Now that you have met all three requirements, I consider you to be a serious Spiritual Warrior ready to do battle "...against the authorities, against the powers of this dark world and against the spiritual forces of evil in the heavenly realms."[4] If this does not describe you, then don't waste your time but pass this book on to someone you think is a serious Spiritual Warrior. If this does describe you and you are ready for some "in your face" training, proceed to Chapter 1.

CHAPTER ONE

The World of Work

WE CHRISTIANS EXPERIENCE the world on two levels. What we can see, touch, hear and smell, I am going to call the physical world. What we experience in our relationships with God and his children, and the forces that struggle against God, I am going to call the spiritual world.

Frank Peretti wrote a couple of books, which capture some of this dualism of experience. In *This Present Darkness*[1], he tells a story at two levels. One level of the story is at the physical level. A story of human events on a college campus. At the second level he describes the spiritual battle between the angel Gabriel and the angels of the devil. The stories are told parallel to one another, and show the underlying spiritual battles between good and evil, which underlie the good and evil at the physical level.

I believe Peretti's novels help sensitize us to the impact of unseen spiritual warfare on our daily life. However, I don't view all the bad things that happen in my workplace at the Florida Department of Health to be the work of the devil, or all of the good to be the result of God. But I do believe that both are present. I believe that the spiritual person does have to live at both levels. I believe that success at the spiritual level will help considerably in struggles at the physical level. I also strongly believe that a person's response to the spiritual warfare must also be at the physical level. That is why many of the solutions to spiritual challenges in the workplace that are presented in this book are in terms of physical behavioral responses. As you will see, the responses that are suggested as responses to spiritual challenges are not to get down on your knees and pray for help, but to do something physically or mentally.

I view the physical world of work as neutral in this discussion of spiritual challenges in the workplace. In this discussion, that actual physical world is not going to help you or hurt you in your effort to be successful in your spiritual challenges.

This discussion is not of the "physical world." As Paul reminds us in Ephesians 6, "(this) struggle is not against flesh and blood, but against the rulers, against the authorities, against the powers of this dark world and against the spiritual forces of evil in the heavenly realm."[2] This discussion is about the spiritual struggle, but in the context of the physical world.

In the physical world I do believe that the workplace can have a negative impact on your spiritual struggles and/or a positive impact. I know of organizations, both private and governmental, that are led by Christians and which create a "Christian friendly work environment." I also speculate that the nature of some business is evil; i.e.

making, promoting and distributing a product that kills people, such as cigarettes. The CEOs of the major tobacco companies recently lied under oath to a committee of Congress, testifying that nicotine was not addictive, even though internal documents stated that the companies were well aware of the addictive power of nicotine.

A company in which the top management openly lies and manufactures a product that kills 400,000 people a year is incompatible with Christian values. Can a person be a Christian and work for a company like that? Yes, but that incompatibility is going to create more spiritual challenges for the Christian than a company that does not have institutional lying and destructive products.

I would hope that individual Christians would include a "Christian friendly" work environment as one requirement as they search for a job.

One reviewer of this manuscript thought my description of the workplace as a jungle made the jungle come across as a negative place. He thought of the jungle as lush exotic environment, full of life. He obviously hasn't lived in the swamps of Florida. In my Ranger training, three weeks of Ranger Operations were spent along the Yellow River at Eglin Air Force Base in the panhandle region of Florida. We were always wet. Insects were incessant. Snakes and alligators were always present. It was not a pleasant place.

In Brace Barber's book, *Ranger School: No Excuse Leadership,* the accounts by individual Rangers of their experiences leaves the reader with strong impressions of how much misery cold weather can inflict, particularly when you are wet. Those in the winter Ranger classes suffered badly from the cold. Thank goodness my class of Ranger School began in July when it was warm. I am so glad that my

Ranger tab is not color coded to indicate what time of the year I went through the course. However, even in the summer, the swamp was generally a hostile environment and a miserable experience.

Armies seldom go into the jungle for pleasure. The missions that take them into the jungle are often dangerous. It is true that the jungle can be a refuge, offering cover from observation and food and water. But I do think of the jungle as a hostile place. That was my experience.

I don't feel that my workplace, Florida Department of Health, is a negative place, but rather a positive place. Many advances in the quality and quantity of life can be contributed to public health through the years. Public Health is a good thing for society and the individual.

So at a physical level, my workplace is a very positive place. At the spiritual level, I do see the workplace as a maze of interactions, events, relationships, people and things that weave a complex matrix, which holds spiritual opportunities as well as dangers. So at this stage of this discussion, please consider the focus to be on the spiritual overlay of the workplace and hold the physical level neutral to the discussion. Consider the spiritual level to be a dangerous jungle, which you need to understand in order to survive and thrive.

CHAPTER TWO

U.S. Army's Teaching on Jungle Danger Areas

IN 1965 THE U.S. Army Ranger School was a "leadership school that used long range patrolling as a teaching vehicle." The course was nine weeks long. The first three weeks were spent at Ft. Benning, Georgia, learning the basics of long range patrolling, a variety of other skills for living and surviving in the jungle, and going through physical conditioning. We were told that our class was the first one to go through the course under a revised curriculum geared to Vietnam. The second three weeks of mountain training was held in the Appalachia National Forest near Dahlonega, Georgia. The third three weeks was spent in the swamps at Eglin Air Force Base out of Auxiliary Field Seven, where General Jimmy Doolittle trained his people for the first bomber raid on Japan.

A grueling conditioning program was a significant part of the Ft. Benning phase. It helped prepare us for walking almost every night to reach and attack an objective at BMNT (Before Morning Nautical Twilight), followed by the return to a base camp only to start again preparing for the next raid. It was said that a Ranger walked about 500 miles during those nine weeks.

Members of the Ranger class were divided into long-range patrols. At some point each student was assigned to be the patrol leader for each of the five components of the long-range patrol. A student had to get a satisfactory performance rating for three out of the five components in order to pass the course. I did graduate, but not without a struggle. Those who graduate receive the coveted Ranger Tab.

Lessons that were pounded into our heads included how to recognize danger areas in the jungle, a course of action to follow if you could not avoid a danger area, and immediate action to take if caught in an ambush in a danger area. Knowing these did not guarantee survival of an enemy attack, but it increased the probability that the patrol would survive and successfully complete the mission.

The teachings about danger areas are a miniscule part of the Ranger School curriculum, but I believe they contain many analogies to the Christian in the world of work. So let me tell you some of the things I learned in Ranger School about jungle danger areas. (**Note:** You can find the specific procedures in the *Ranger Handbook*.[1] This is available through www.amazon.com)

The Ranger Handbook defines danger areas as follows

> A danger area (DA) is any place on a unit's route where the leader's estimate process tells him his unit may be exposed to enemy observation or fire. Some examples of danger areas are open areas, roads and trails, native villages, enemy positions, and obstacles such as minefields, streams, and barbed wire. Avoid danger areas whenever possible. If they must be passed or crossed, use great caution.[2]

Trails, roads, streams, clear areas and ridge-tops are danger areas. Stay off them! Why are they danger areas? Because these are the easiest ways to get through the jungle, and ambushers know that solders like to take the easy path. Hey Spiritual Warrior, can you already see the analogy to the Christian in the workplace? It is human nature to want to take the easy path through any circumstance, whether it is through a thick jungle, administrative procedures, human relationships, or moral dilemmas in the workplace.

Sometimes a long-range patrol could not avoid a danger area. Then the Ranger School taught procedures or protocols to negotiate the danger area in such a way as to minimize the danger to the patrol and its mission. For example, if a patrol was moving along a compass azimuth that would lead to its objective, and the word came back to the patrol leader that the point man had come across a road running 90 degrees left and right to the patrol's direction of movement, you knew that you had encountered a danger area. See Diagram #1.

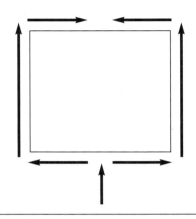

Road (A Danger Area)

Left
Security

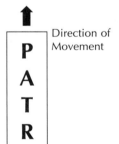

Direction of
Movement

Right
Security

P
A
T
R
O
L

Diagram 1

The following is the Ranger School protocol for dealing with this danger area. The patrol leader first establishes security on the left and right of the patrol up on the road. This usually meant putting an M–60 machine gun at each location. These members of the patrol would block attack from either direction along the road while the patrol crossed the road.

The patrol leader would then send a party across the road to "box out" the area the patrol would be entering when it crossed the road. The purpose of this process was to insure that there was no enemy in the area the patrol would be entering as they crossed the road. This involved several men crossing the road and then going in different directions. One team would go to the left 50 meters, while the other would go 50 meters to the right. At the end of the 50 meters, each team would turn 90 degrees and go 50 meters in the direction of movement. At the end of those 50 meters, each team would turn 90 degrees and turn toward each other, closing the box. Some of the team would remain in the cleared area while word was sent back to the main body of the patrol that the area was clear of the enemy.

With security to the left and right of the patrol on the road, and the area to be entered on the other side of the road clear, the patrol leader would then move the patrol across the road as quickly and quietly as possible.

This detailed scenario is provided to convey an understanding of how much time and effort has been expended by military trainers in order to insure success of a mission with the least possible causality. The analogy here is that Christians can and should develop strategies for successful Christian living through difficult situations before they happen.[3]

Another pre-established protocol used by the Ranger patrol is one for breaking contact with the enemy. Again from the Ranger Handbook:

> Break Contact (Platoon/Squad). Squad/platoon is moving and the enemy fires on the unit. Squad/platoon leader orders unit to break contact.
>
> 1. The leader gives the order to break contact.
> 2. The leader designates which element will be the support element, and which element will move to initiate the break in contact. For a squad, the initial support element will usually be a fire team (half a squad) and the initial movement element will be a fire team. For a platoon (four squads), it will be a squad.
> 3. The squad/platoon leader orders a distance and direction of movement, such as "nine o'clock, Hill Top," to move.
> 4. The support element increases the rate of fire to suppress the enemy."[4]

Pre-established protocols are critical and are as important for the Spiritual Warrior as to the Army Ranger on long-range patrols.

As a Christian you should not wait until you come under fire or encounter a spiritual danger area to think up what you are going to do. Most of the spiritual dangers areas you face in your workplace can be anticipated, as can most of the spiritual attacks you experience.

In Ranger School, one of the underlying principles taught, which is a critical component of all of the Ranger's field protocols, is to know where you are on the map at all times. This facilitates the resumption of your mission after a break in contact with the enemy, or when negotiating an unavoidable danger area.

In 1965, there was no operational Global Positioning System (GPS) available to the Ranger. (Note: GPS is a system of navigation fed by satellites to a hand held receiver that gives the person on the ground his exact location in latitude and longitude.) The Ranger's navigational tools were primarily topographical maps, the compass, and measured courses used to establish the number of paces in a hundred meters over different terrain.

If the mission required the patrol to walk "five clicks" (five kilometers, 1.6 KM in one mile) to an objective that night, the patrol leader would determine his current location on a topographical map, and plot the azimuth(s) to the objective. After he reconned the objective during daylight, he would brief the patrol on the mission and always orient the patrol to the course to and from the objective.

One patrol member was always appointed to be responsible for keeping up with the distance. That person would usually have a small rope in which he would place a knot at the end of each 500 meters. He would keep the patrol leader informed at the end of each kilometer, and more often as the patrol approached the objective.

Underlying all long range patrolling was the basic requirement that every member of the patrol would know where he was on the map at all times. This was critical if there was a need to break contact from the enemy or if, for whatever reason, the patrol leader had to be replaced by another member of the patrol. As you will see later, knowing where you are when you plan a mission and knowing where you are all of the time during a mission has important implications for the success of the Spiritual Warrior.

Hey reader, let me show you something about land navigation that has implications for you as a Spiritual Warrior.

In Diagram #2 you see a topographical map that has six hilltops separated by a ridge.

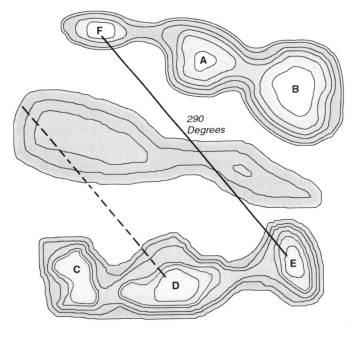

Diagram 2

You want to go to mountaintop F. From your observations you have determined that you are on mountaintop E. Using your protractor you plot an azimuth and find that you need to follow your compass on a reading of 260 degrees from your current location. According to your topographic map, mountaintop F is five kilometers away. If you follow your compass heading and go 5 clicks you will find the rest of your patrol on mountaintop F.

So night comes and you lead your patrol on a course of 260 degrees. You can't see mountaintop F but you trust your map and compass and head out into the dark along the solid line. Hey Spiritual Warrior, didn't I tell you Rangers always walked at night, every night, all night. It turns out your map was right, your compass was right, you followed your azimuth correctly, but your actual course was the broken line.

You never reached mountaintop F because your starting point was not mountaintop E. You actually started from mountaintop D. You did not start from where you thought you were. This leads to a very important principle of land navigation, which is also true for spiritual warfare. It is important to know where you are going, but it is more important to know where you are. In a hostile jungle you need to know where you are 24/7 (24 hours a day, 7 days a week), because there is no telling when you are going to need to go in a direction that requires a correct starting point.

It is more important to know where you are than where you are going! In ranger school it is critical that you know your current location relative to the ground at all times. In life it is critical that you know your current location relative to God at all times.

Hey Spiritual Warrior, do you know where you are in your relationship with God? Do you know where you are in relationship to God all the time (24/7)? This leads us to a corollary: Do not voluntarily enter a spiritual danger area if you do not know where you are spiritually!

CHAPTER THREE

The Bible's Teaching on Spiritual Danger Areas

THE MORE I TALKED with others about the application of the teaching of the Ranger School on danger areas in the jungle to the spiritual danger areas Christians face in the workplace, the more aware I became of the military model that Paul used to teach the principles of successful Christian warfare. No scripture captures this more than Ephesians 6. Please read the following in its entirety, even though you may already be familiar with it.

Ephesians 6:[1]

> Be strong in the Lord and in his mighty power. Put on the full armor of God so that you can take your stand against the devil's schemes. For our struggle is not against flesh and blood, but against the rulers, against the authorities, against the powers of this dark world and against the spiritual forces of evil in the heavenly realms. Therefore put on the full armor of God, so that

when the day of evil comes, you may be able to stand your ground, and after you have done everything, to stand. Stand firm then, with the **belt of truth** buckled around your waist, with the **breastplate of righteousness** in place. And with your **feet fitted** with the readiness that comes from the gospel of peace. In addition to all this, take up the **shield of faith,** with which you can extinguish all the flaming arrows of the evil one. Take the **helmet of salvation** and the **sword of the Spirit,** which is the word of God. And pray in the Spirit on all occasions with all kinds of prayers and requests.[2]

Hey, Spiritual Warrior, I don't want to pop your bubble, but that ain't enough. Arming yourself with weapons and armor is not enough!

Paul would have been wrong if that were as far as he went. But Thank You God, Paul did not stop there. Read the next sentence:

With this in mind, be alert and always keep on praying for all the saints.[3]

Did Paul say, "Be alert"? No! Paul said,

BE ALERT!!

In all the hundreds of times that I have read Ephesians 6, I don't think I ever saw the "be alert" before. I know I never saw it as I do now.

Peter reinforces Paul's admonition in 1 Peter 5:8. "Be self-controlled and alert. Your enemy the devil prowls around like a roaring lion looking for someone to devour."

Hey Spiritual Warrior, Paul had his problems with sin, things that separated him from God. In Romans he says,

> ...I am unspiritual, sold as a slave to sin. I do not understand what I do. For what I want to do I do not do, but what I hate I do....I know that nothing good lives in me, that is in my sinful nature. For I have the desire to do what is good, but I cannot carry it out. For what I do is not the good I want to do; no, the evil I do not want to do-this I keep on doing. Now if I do what I do not want to do, it is no longer I who do it, but it is sin living in me that does it.[4]

No matter how hard you try, you will always be more human than you are spiritual. That was true for Paul. That is true of me and that is true of you! In my opinion, Jesus is the only man ever to be more spiritual than human, and even he had his problems with things that would separate Him from God. Remember in the Garden of Gethsemane, he knew what God the Father wanted him to do but he didn't want to do it. He even prayed that he would not be required to do it. I believe even in that situation Jesus had a choice. He consciously chose to do God's will. He consciously of his own free will chose the Cross.

Being human is not bad. God made us that way! He did not make us automatons that would automatically do his will. God wants us to have free choice. That is God's plan for man.

Because of the way God made man, every opportunity to sin requires conscious choice to sin or not to sin. You will never be so holy that you can't sin. Stop looking for a relationship with God that is so pure that it will always compel you to do what is Godly without your having to think about it. You will never have that this side of heaven. Thinking that way is how the "evil forces" sucker you into doing things that separate you from God. Don't expect that you can be so spiritual and so indwelled with the Holy Spirit, that you are permanently inoculated from sin. There are no vaccines to protect you from sin.

Every spiritual challenge, which is an opportunity to sin, requires a conscious choice. To make the "right choice" the Spiritual Warrior, must first recognize that he is at a decision point. That requires being alert 24/7. Being alert is what this book is all about!

The spiritual solder must be well equipped by wearing the full armor of God: the belt of truth, the breastplate of righteousness, shoes of readiness, the shield of faith, and the helmet of salvation. The spiritual solder must know and be able to use his weapon, the sword of the spirit. But Paul says these are not enough. In the last sentence Paul says that after you've done all of this, and are well equipped and know how and are able to use your weapon, BE ALERT!

Being alert is a warning not to get ambushed. Paul knew that the spiritual enemies do not play fair. It is a major spiritual insight to not let your guard down while you are cutting your way through the spiritual jungle. This is particularly true when you are out in the world working yourself through the jungle of the workplace. Being able to recognize spiritual danger areas will help you BE ALERT. Paul is telling the Spiritual Warrior to be watchful.

My goal with this book is to describe some of the spiritual danger areas that may be found in the world of work with such specificity, that the alert, well prepared, and armed, confident, serious Spiritual Warrior can recognize them immediately and accurately, just like the Ranger recognizes a road he comes across as he cuts his way through the jungle as a danger area. The Spiritual Warrior will see these danger areas for what they are, opportunities of vulnerability to the schemes of the devil.

I hope this book will make you aware that the jungle of the workplace holds many danger areas. I hope it will help you to know the kinds of things you need to be watchful for, and to know in advance how to respond to those danger areas. I also hope this book will help you become sensitive to other danger areas that may be in your personal workplace jungle, and help you be able to develop effective protocols for dealing with them.

CHAPTER FOUR

Spiritual Danger Areas Defined

I BELIEVE THAT once you enter into a personal relationship with God, you are "born again," "saved," "converted," whatever you want to call it, and that it is a permanent relationship. It is similar to your relationship with your parents. Once you are born into their family you will always be their son or daughter. No matter what you do, that cannot change. You can do things that hurt them, you can move far away from them physically, ethically, emotionally, etc., but you will always be their child.

However, although we can never sever our relationship with God, we can separate ourselves from God. We can impair that relationship. We can do things that break that fellowship with God. Those things that come between God and us, we call sin. Sin separates us from God. Anything that separates you from God is sin! That is what happened in the Garden of Eden. Man walked away from God and his fellowship by choosing to do something that God said not to do. Eating the forbidden fruit separated man from God. Eating the forbidden fruit was sin because God said don't eat the fruit.

In preparation for writing this book, I interviewed mature Christians. I asked them to identify situations, people, and ideas they have confronted in the workplace that have challenged their personal relationship with God. These I call spiritual danger areas. I then asked them to help me identify what they had done when they were confronted by these situations that had helped them be successful in staying faithful to their personal relationship to God. More specifically, I asked them when they couldn't avoid these spiritually challenging situations, what actions did they take to successfully deal with them. I call these actions "protocols." Through these conversations, I was able to identify eight spiritual danger areas.

A spiritual danger area is a situation, a place, a person, or a thought that makes us vulnerable to doing things that separate us from God. The serious confident Christian needs to be alert for those events, and have a plan to deal with them, before he finds himself in a spiritual danger area.

If a spiritual danger area is a place where something could happen that would separate you from God, and anything that separates you from God is called sin, then your approach to a spiritual danger area is your approach to sin. This book therefore presents a philosophy for dealing with sin. It is my hope you will come away with a highly defined sense of how to approach sin.

Most of us go through the day without major emergencies. As the Administrative Officer in the Office of Emergency Operations, Florida Department of Health, I spend a lot of time around people who have made it their life to deal with emergencies. You may know some of these types. They quickly recognize emergencies, and they are never at a loss as to what to do. They have been there before!

Most of us have a hard time even recognizing that we are in an emergency, much less having a clue as to what we should do. The goal of this book is to sensitize you to recognizing spiritual danger areas in the workplace and to provide examples of pre-established protocols for dealing with these in such a way that you will not let what happens in a spiritual danger area penetrate and break down your personal relationship with God.

There is a difference between knowledge and skill.

I remember when my son, John, got his learner's permit to drive. He wanted to drive the moment we walked out the door of the testing station. I told him we would wait until we got to Dancer's Image, a quite side street beside our house.

I stopped the car as soon as we turned on to Dancer's Image and swapped places with John.

"OK John, let me tell you how to drive the car!"

John looked at me incredulously and said, "I KNOW how to drive."

John let out the clutch. The car lurched and lurched, stopping and starting with violent jerks for 50 feet before the engine died. This happened four times before we got to the end of the block. He became more and more open to my suggestion that he release the clutch slowly as he pressed on the gas.

John knew how to drive before he sat in the driver's seat. But he had little driving skills in the beginning, although the skills quickly came. This is an example of the difference between knowledge and skill. A skill is knowledge applied well!

As a Christian we sometimes fail to understand the difference in the **knowledge** required to live a Christian Life, and the **skills** required to put that knowledge into practice. Just because you know it doesn't mean you can do it! So, Spiritual Warrior, how do you get that skill to do what you know?

You practice what you preach. Hey Spiritual Warrior, have you ever hear that before? One military veteran stated that if you can't do it in training you will never be able to do it for real. The problem with the training is that there is not much of a way to practice these spiritual principles but in the real situation. By its nature, spiritual war is real all of the time. So look at every minute as an opportunity to put these principles into play. Over time you will develop the skills.

You might find a spiritual mentor in your workplace. A more mature Spiritual Warrior who can be a source of counsel and support.

An alternative might be a fellow Spiritual Warrior equivalent to the Ranger Buddy in Ranger School.

In Ranger School you did everything with that Ranger Buddy. Anytime you were separated from your Ranger Buddy, he knew where you were. Each held the other accountable. The Ranger Buddy helped you when you needed help. No one on the Ranger Long Range Patrol cared or promoted your success more than your Ranger Buddy.

In the workplace one needs a spiritual warrior "buddy" to do spiritually what the Ranger Buddy did for the Ranger. I think of that "buddy" more as a colleague than a mentor.

There is more of a sense that we are in this together and we are going to successfully survive the jungle and accomplish our mission. Hey Spiritual Warrior, do you have a spiritual ranger buddy at work? If not, get one!!

WARNING: The skill of living your faith in the workplace is as distinct and separate from being a Christian, as is knowing how to drive and being able to drive. Some of our fellow Christians think that just because they are a Christian and the Holy Spirit lives in them that they have taken care of business. **In the presence of sin, it is irresponsible to think that the Holy Spirit will compel you to do the "Christian thing" without your making a conscious choice and effort.** This side of heaven, you will always be more human than spiritual.

CHAPTER FIVE

Eight Spiritual Danger Areas

I HAVE TRIED to describe each of the following spiritual danger areas in such a manner so that they would be as recognizable to the Spiritual Warrior in the workplace as a road encountered in a jungle by a Ranger on a long-range patrol.

For example, you are walking through the jungle and come across a road. It should hit you in the face that you have encountered a danger area. The encounter with the road has triggered an alert that should start your implementation of the preplanned protocol you have for that danger area.

Many of the danger areas in the workplace are not as obvious or recognizable as a road or trail in the jungle. These danger areas are often mental. The workplace jungle is office routine, paper work, and a horde of people with whom you must interact. Your spiritual danger areas are hidden in all of that.

So to help you recognize spiritual danger areas, you need to explicitly define triggers or **red flags** that will prompt you into action. You must first recognize the spiritual danger area. Then you match a predetermined response to that danger area, and do whatever is called for by the protocol. You just do it!

A correct response to a spiritual danger area does not require inspiration, it requires discipline!

This book does not contain a comprehensive list of spiritual danger areas. The danger areas included are certainly not all of the danger areas that the Spiritual Warrior is going to face in the workplace. These eight spiritual danger areas are only representative of what you might encounter in your spiritual jungle. The spiritual danger areas presented may not even be in your jungle. Or you may not have encountered them yet, since some are more likely to be experienced later in a person's work career than at the beginning.

A soldier does not have to know if a road is paved or just a dirt road to know that it is a danger area when he comes across it in the jungle. It isn't necessary to know what kind of traffic may pass on the road to know that a road is an ideal place to be ambushed. I'm saying this in part to help you understand that you will not find a lot of in-depth explanation or analysis as to why the following spiritual danger areas are dangerous to your personal relationship to God. In order to protect your relationship with God, all you need to do is recognize that an area is spiritually dangerous, and then respond as you have predetermined to respond.

The protocols identified here are not the only responses one might use, but they have also been found to work. The key idea in the development and use of protocols is that you have a predetermined response to recognized spiritual danger areas. It is my hope that you will use the following as a starting point to identify the spiritual danger areas in your workplace, and the protocols that work for you. To enter the same danger area a second time without an alert trigger to help you recognize it and a protocol to deal with it is not smart. In fact, it is dumb! The dumb ranger who cannot learn from his mistakes will not survive the ambushes that wait for him in the jungle.

SPIRITUAL DANGER AREA—Something More

Description

Interactions with the opposite sex that have the potential for inappropriate sexual and/or emotional relations.

Discussion

For the Christian, sexual intercourse is proper only when it is between a man and a woman who are married to each other. The Bible is explicit on this standard. Married Christians must be particularly alert to interactions that could lead to inappropriate relations, but this may not be a danger area in the same way for single people who are free to marry. In fact, I would hope there would be no move toward marriage unless both parties feel that "something more" is possible. This discussion of this danger area is limited to situations when one or both people are married to someone else.

Physical relationships between single people are fraught with their own spiritual danger areas. Single people need to decide what is an appropriate level of physical relationship for them when they begin to court or be courted by a potential spouse, and in casual dating as well. Holding hands may be wrong for some. For others kissing may be OK. After engagement more intimate physical activity, short of intercourse, may be appropriate. But the biggest warning here is to decide before you encounter those situations how to recognize it as a danger area and know in advance how you are going to deal with it.

With more and more women in management positions in work organizations, there is more and more interaction between the sexes on routine business matters. If the focus is kept on the business at hand, these interactions are not spiritual danger areas. So when does it become a spiritual danger area? As one interviewee stated, "It is too late once the two of you are standing naked in a motel room." Somewhere between a simple business interaction with a person of the opposite sex, and "standing naked in a motel room," the Christian has encountered, entered and succumbed to this spiritual danger.

Examples

Flirting: Men and women are attracted to each other for a variety of reasons. It is pleasurable emotionally and physically. It may be eye contact or suggestive comments that imply an attraction that leads to the conclusion that you, and or the other party, is interested in "something more" than just talking about business.

A Person: A specific person to whom you are attracted and who is married to another person may be a specific danger area to be avoided.

Business Trips, Out of Town Conferences and Conventions: A danger area may exist when members of the opposite sex travel together out of town on business.

A Place: I believe that President Clinton is a born again Christian. However, from all accounts, one of his spiritual danger areas was a windowless hallway that led to the Oval Office. If he could not avoid such a place, he should have never been there with a woman other than his wife. For King David, the roof of his palace became a spiritual danger area for him when Bathsheba was taking a bath on the roof of her house.[1]

ALERT TRIGGER You feel the chemistry. The endorphins flow. For males it's often sexual arousal; for females it may also be an emotional attraction. When asked to define pornography, Supreme Court Justice Potter Stewart said, "I know it when I see it!"

These feelings can occur during business and work encounters. This is normal and natural. It may be OK for single people, although this kind of involvement in the workplace also has its spiritual dangers for them. It is a RED ALERT if one or both are married to other people.

ALERT TRIGGER A person who "turns you on."
As a married Christian, when you see a person to whom you are attracted and vulnerable, you should be alerted that you are walking into a danger area. Keep your guard up!

ALERT TRIGGER Hiding a relationship.
Feeling that you need to hide a relationship or encounter with an individual from others should be an alert. The need for a Christian to hide a relationship with someone of the opposite sex is sure evidence that it is not proper, and that it is a spiritual danger area.

ALERT TRIGGER Men and women on the same trip.
Isolated from the family setting, this can be seductive and subtle.

Protocol for Victorious Action

Protocol 1: Divert the discussion away from the personal to the business. Refer positively to your spouse and family. Find ways to indicate that there is no way that there is going to be "something more" between the two of you.

Protocol 2: Have pictures of spouse and family in your office. Have a Bible on your desk or bookcase. Let your office environment announce, no, let your office shout to the world that you are taken and not interested in "something more" with anyone other than your spouse.

Protocol 3: Avoid that specific person to whom you are inappropriately attracted. I've joked in the past that one of the most important lessons I learned in the hand-to-hand combat training in Ranger School was knowing when to run. Have you ever been in a struggle when the opposing forces were overwhelming? When that is the case, retreating is the best strategy if surviving is important to the mission. This chemistry between men and women can be overwhelming. When that happens, get out of the situation. Run, Run, Run!

Note to the Spiritual Warrior: *After reading through this first spiritual danger area do you get the idea? The alert that you are in or entering this danger area is that "feeling" that either of you are interested in something more. That is the **red flag**, and should trigger an immediate disciplined response.*

47

SPIRITUAL DANGER AREA—The Angry Other

Description

In an interaction with another person, the other person is getting angry with you.

Discussion

Day to day interactions with other people are not necessarily spiritual danger areas. However, when another person becomes angry with you, for whatever the reason, it is a spiritual danger area capable of disrupting your personal relationship with God. The angry person may be a customer, an employee, a co-worker, or a supervisor. Anyone who requires an interaction in order to do business may become angry with you or the situation. You may not be able to stop the other person's anger, but you can be disciplined in your response. You can respond in such a way that your spiritual self overcomes and is victorious. You can handle it in such a way that your relationship with God directs your response.

Examples

A customer returns an item recently purchased because it unexpectedly broke. The customer is upset when he walks in the door, in part because his expectations about the product and what you told him about the product were different from his experience. Another example may be in a governmental agency when a staff member followed your directions in handling a transaction, and the results were not positive, as you had led the staff member to expect. Many times anger comes from failed expectations.

ALERT TRIGGER   The other person becomes angry.

Protocol for Victorious Action

Concentrate on treating the other person the way you would want to be treated. This may take the concentration and focus of a wide receiver who has run his pass pattern and gotten hit every time, feet knocked out from under him, and the wind knocked out of him. Yet he has to run that pattern again with discipline, knowing that if he does it right, he will be in the right place at the right time when the ball is thrown to him. In spite of abusive language from the other person, and their unfair and incorrect statements, you must be disciplined in your focus to treat that other person the way you would want to be treated.

Note to the Spiritual Warrior: *Becoming angry yourself is as much or more of a spiritual danger area as the "angry other." That is a danger area not developed here but should be developed by a Spiritual Warrior who has a problem with his own anger.*

SPIRITUAL DANGER AREA—Small Things

Description

Minor tasks or events involving values, ethics, or convictions that are performed in isolation, or with little supervision, and that require some judgment.

Discussion

On the day I interviewed the individual who first brought up small things as a danger area, the headlines of the Tallahassee Democrat (our local newspaper) announced that a former Speaker of the Florida House of Representatives had been indicted for tax fraud. The interviewee stated that the Speaker's problems did not begin with defrauding the government of taxes; it began with much smaller things. He shared that his experience had been that people who show up in high profile crime began by cutting corners on little things. It was the lack of discipline in little things that led to larger infractions.

Examples

Travel Vouchers: Often there is work-related travel. Every organization has some procedure to authorize travel and reimburse the employees for their travel. Amounts are often small, but can be large if air travel or extended stays in hotels are involved. In most organizations the individual initiates the travel reimbursement request. The request for reimbursement is often an opportunity to "fudge." Authorization for certain meals or per deim may require departure times before a given hour. In Florida government at the state level, a person must leave for a trip prior to 6:00 AM in order to qualify for full per diem for that day.

The Spiritual Warrior will be completely honest about the departure time, regardless of qualification for per diem. That is a small thing, but one which the evil forces can use to ambush the true believer.

Log of Time Worked: Time worked is reported periodically for purposes of computing one's pay and leave. Most employees keep a log of their time. That is a small thing.

Use of Copiers and Faxes for Personal Business: Using copiers and fax machines at work for personal reasons is another "small thing" that can compromise a Christian's witness and walk with God.

Taking Office Supplies for Personal Use: Pencils, pens, paper clips, pads of paper are examples of small things that can find their way home with Christians, as well as non-Christian workers.

ALERT TRIGGER You may be thinking that this is "no big deal." Each one is a small thing. Key words may also trigger an alert of vulnerability and spiritual danger, such as "Travel Voucher," "Time Log" or "No Big Deal."

Protocol for Victorious Action

Time Logs: Keep a daily time log at your desk or location where you start and end your workday. Record the time in a daily log the first thing when arriving at your desk, and the last thing when leaving for the day. Use that time for your time log, not an estimate of the time you arrived in the parking lot. If you forget to record your leaving time, and remember that you failed to record that time when you get out to your car, write that time down on something you will have with you the next day; i.e., a day planner. Don't estimate stop and start times. Use actual times. The devil just loves to get Christians to hedge on the truth.

Absolute truth is the Christian's goal, absolute truth about yourself. You have nothing to hide. The dark world of the devil loves deception. The Christian needs to be open and above board in all things. No matter the angle, when the non-Christian world is looking at you, it should see no deception, no chinks in the armor, especially in regard to the small things.

SPIRITUAL DANGER AREA—Conflict of Interest

Description

Any decision or action from which I benefit in money, position, and/or influence that results in a negative outcome to the work organization, a colleague, or a customer.

Discussion

Any transaction in the workplace from which you will personally benefit has the potential of being a conflict of interest. Situations that have a "conflict" of interest are analogous to a zero sum game. That is, in order for you to benefit or gain, another party has to lose. Those situations are dangerous to your spiritual well being. In his book, Reality Therapy, Dr. William Glasser defined responsible behavior as behavior in which the individual meets his needs without keeping others from meeting their own needs. According to Glasser, there is an element of irresponsible behavior in decisions and actions which creates conflicts of interest. You benefit while others or the organization, or both, are harmed.

There is probably a hierarchy of conflicts of interest in work organizations. Conflicts of interest that are experienced by beginning workers, or workers at lower levels in the organization, will often have limited consequences to the well being of the work organization and/or personal benefits to them. But even the smallest conflict of interest can have a major impact on the spiritual well being of the individuals involved.

Examples

Your company has a contract to develop a curriculum for a proposed new medical school. In the age of managed care, a modern medical curriculum would be incomplete without some introduction to managed care. This would necessarily include involvement of one of the largest health care organizations in the area in training students or involving students in managed care. However, you've been associated with the Board of Directors of the health care organization from its inception. You and the HMO will benefit by inclusion of the HMO in the medical school curriculum.

ALERT TRIGGER   I benefit!

Protocol for Victorious Action

Avoid conflicts of interest if at all possible. If they cannot be avoided, modify the circumstances so that you do not benefit personally. If avoiding or modifying this danger area is not possible, first talk through the situation with a trusted friend who will be objective and will help you see the real conflicts. Be open about the real conflicts with the significant parties so that there is no appearance that any benefits you may experience are being hidden. Involve all the significant parties in the process to determine if there is indeed a conflict of interest.

For example, in the previous illustration the "real reason" for including managed care in the potential medical school curriculum may be that it primarily benefits the client (University), and not you or your company, or the HMO. In this particular situation, a meeting was called with the contractor, the President of the University, and Medical Director of the HMO.

After explaining the concern, the President of the University declared that including the HMO in the managed care curriculum for the medical school was not a conflict of interest, but of "mutual interest" to both parties. He approved the inclusion of the HMO in the curriculum. (Note: Subsequent revisions of the plan deleted that section of the recommended curriculum.)

SPIRITUAL DANGER AREA—Transitions

Description

A significant change in geographical location or organizational position.

Discussion

We only have so much emotional energy available to deal with life. Sometimes we do not realize all that is going on can deplete that energy and make us spiritually vulnerable. Some of those times when we are most vulnerable are times when we are in transition.

During transition times we are having to deal with a lot of unknowns. We are out of our routine and required to think and deal with many things that we ordinarily do not have to confront. These additional things become distractions that cause us to divert our attention. When we take our eyes off of events that have spiritual implications we become spiritually vulnerable.

Examples

You graduate from college or complete that graduate degree. The period between school and beginning work can be full of energy demanding surprises. Your company has reassigned you in the same job to a different location. You've been promoted to a new position working with different people and different programs within the same business.

There are often many new experiences during transitions. New experiences are not necessarily bad, but our bodies and emotions do react. Often we interpret these new experiences as bad and go into either the "fight" or "flight" mode, neither of which may be warranted.

ALERT TRIGGER   Change of jobs. Change of communities.

Protocol for Victorious Action

During transitions, focus on family relationships. Overly dwell and participate in family activities at every opportunity. Encourage growth toward one another. Guard against separations that could undermine family relationships. Those relationships will provide identity and known stability during uncertain periods of transition when the bedrock of your life seems to be shifting.

SPIRITUAL DANGER AREA—Spiritual Overconfidence

Description

The determination that you don't need to read the Bible, pray regularly, attend worship or Bible study, or tithe are indicators of spiritual overconfidence. If this is true of you, you may be spiritually overconfident.

Discussion

The emerging of spiritual overconfidence is like the process of your eyeglasses getting dirty. You don't realize your glasses are dirty until they are too dirty for you to see through them clearly. Others may notice that your glasses need cleaning before you do. Glasses get dirty gradually; and our vision tends to adjust to this impairment.[1]

Another way to put this is that you have begun to feel comfortable walking through the jungle. You have no sense of danger because you feel you can handle anything that the "authorities, the powers of the dark world and the spiritual forces of evil in the heavenly realms" can throw at you. Do you feel spiritually invincible in the workplace? If you answer "yes," you may be spiritually overconfident.

You may feel more comfortable in the world because you have relaxed your standards. There may be a false sense of overconfidence because you have watered down your idea of what it is to be a Christian. Your standard cannot be the Christians around you, but your own maximum relationship with God. That is the standard against which you should measure your spirituality.

Examples

You look at other Christians and believe that you are "more Christian" than they are. You've just written a book telling Christians how to be better Christians. That is prima facia evidence that you think you know more about this than others. In that case you may be wallowing in a spiritual danger area.

| **ALERT TRIGGER** | The feeling of spiritual invincibility or spiritual superiority over other Christians. |

Protocol for Victorious Action

Focus on your relationship with God. Acknowledge to God that your relationship to him is his gift, which you enjoy only by his grace. You've done nothing to earn it. To avoid this danger area: participate in weekly worship and maintain your daily disciplines of Bible study and prayer. This is like cleaning your glasses periodically, regardless of whether or not you think they need it.

SPIRITUAL DANGER AREA—Authority and Power

Description

A position in the work organization with discretionary authority to direct people and/or resources.

Discussion

There is a difference between authority and power in work organizations. Authority is legitimate responsibilities that accompany a recognized position on the organizational chart. Power to influence decisions, staff, and resources may be found in people who do not necessarily occupy a position of authority.

Power may come from being at the intersection of information that is critical to the organization. Control of information critical to the work organization may sometime be in the hands of staff at the lower levels of the organization.

Having authority and or organizational power is not necessarily bad. It is the potential use of the authority and/or power that creates opportunities that may be used for the good of the organization and others, or for the good of the individual and harmful to the organization. That makes them spiritual danger areas. Often individuals are attracted to people who have organizational authority and/or power because of their own self-interest.

Several interviewees stated that some women find authority and power held by men to be an aphrodisiac. This is a double danger area, a layering of danger areas one on another. Be doubly vigilant when you find yourself in a double danger area.

Examples

You are a manager of staff. In every decision or direction you can tailor the result so that you will benefit personally. A standard for a manager in decisions affecting resources is to avoid those that result in enhancing your position. I have known managers in state government who never did anything unless they personally got something out of it. People like this are easy to spot and are usually well known within the organization.

That approach to management undermines your testimony as one of God's Spiritual Warriors. This can also happen with lower level employees who are given new responsibilities that allow them to control resources or team responsibilities. They can let this go to their head, get a big head, and take an approach that primarily enhances their position in the organization.

Remember, self-sacrifice was the hallmark of Jesus.

ALERT TRIGGER You have the authority to tell others what to do. You have the authority to decide how to spend money. You have organizational power to force others to act or spend the way you direct. You are in a Spiritual Danger Area.

Protocol for Victorious Action

Make decisions or give directions that result in a positive impact for the work organization and the individuals involved, and that also have minimal gains to you. The appearance of an ulterior motive may be as bad as the real thing for the Spiritual Warrior.

SPIRITUAL DANGER AREA—Fatigue

Description

"Fatigue: a condition of impairment, resulting from prolonged mental or physical activity or both, usually removable by rest."[2] You know it if you've got it. When you are fatigued you are in a spiritual danger area.

Discussion

Vince Lombardi, the legendary coach of the Green Bay Packers, is reported to have said, "Fatigue makes cowards of us all!" What is it about that fatigue that makes us vulnerable to spiritual attack? In my opinion we become spiritually vulnerable because we lose our focus and concentration. Our reaction time for recognizing spiritual danger is decreased.

Examples

You have often felt this level of fatigue. You know it physically and mentally. You know you are not operating at your peak. Many late night study sessions have made you aware that you can push your body and mind to extraordinary extremes. But have you always been aware that you are also putting yourself at risk spiritually?

ALERT TRIGGER Probably the best alert trigger to this danger area is the physiology of fatigue. You feel extremely tired. You feel extremely sleepy. You may also become very "loose emotionally," finding it easy to cry over things that you would not when rested. Listen to your body. It is telling you that it needs rest. Redefine those feelings to include the spiritual danger you are in.

Protocol for Victorious Action

If you can't avoid this danger area then go to great lengths to focus on the spiritual threats that come your way. Obviously the best protocol is go to bed and get rested!

CHAPTER SIX

Conclusions

ARE THE IDEAS presented here so obvious that they seem trivial and of no interest to the Christian? Some Christians seem to think so. It is those Christians who seem to trip over the obvious, right into a spiritual ambush. Because they were slow to recognize the spiritual danger area or had no plan to deal with the danger area, they faltered, damaging their personal relationship with God and undermining their ministry and testimony in the workplace. **Remember Spiritual Warrior, a correct response to a spiritual danger area does not require inspiration, it requires discipline!**

I am not talking about ethical behavior. I am talking about the behavior of a true Spiritual Warrior. A non-Christian can be ethical in his behavior. Many are. A Christian Warrior's behavior is driven by his relationship with God. Nothing is more precious to the Christian Warrior than that relationship. He will defend it and protect it to the end.

It is that relationship that must be in all that he does. Someone said that a watertight ship can sail in any storm on any ocean. For the Spiritual Warrior, that water tightness comes from his relationship with God. What the Spiritual Warrior puts at jeopardy when he enters an unavoidable spiritual danger area is separation from God. The "evil forces" cannot sever that relationship, but they can cause separation from God. The protocols describe what the Spiritual Warrior can do that will result in maintaining his close relationship to God.

Ephesians 6 makes it very plain that the Christian is involved in spiritual warfare. The uninformed, apathetic, undisciplined, uncommitted, and unprepared Christian who blunders into a spiritual danger area is subject to the withering assault of the "evil forces," just as much as the flesh and blood soldier who breaks out of the jungle into a danger area and right into an ambush. WAKE UP CHRISTIAN WARRIOR!!

BE ALERT! Look for spiritual danger areas. Avoid danger areas you see ahead. Know your protocols for significant spiritual danger areas you know you will face. That is, know what you are going to do when you find yourself confronted with an unavoidable spiritual danger area. Be disciplined in your response to those in which you find yourself. In so doing you will not only survive the spiritual jungle of the workplace, but also be victorious over each one that challenges you!

IDENTIFY YOUR SPIRITUAL DANGER AREAS IN THE WORKPLACE

I've included a worksheet in Appendix D to help identify the spiritual dangers you are facing in your workplace.

Don't put this book down without filling out that sheet. Identify just one spiritual danger area. If it is not one of the areas that's been discussed, could it be gossip or jealousy, maybe laziness or just not doing your best? This worksheet may be a step toward more victorious Christian living on your job.

SUMMARY OF INSIGHTS

- Becoming a Christian is hard to understand but easy to do. Being a Christian is easy to understand but hard to do! Page 11

- It is more important to know where you are than where you are going! Page 31

- Although we can never sever our relationship with God, we can separate ourselves from God. Page 37

- A spiritual danger area is a situation, a place, a person, or a thought that makes us vulnerable to doing things that separate us from God. Page 38

- It is irresponsible, in the presence of sin, to think that the Holy Spirit will compel you to do the "Christian thing" without your making a conscious choice and effort. Page 41

- A correct response to a spiritual danger area does not require inspiration, it requires discipline! Page 43

- Faith does not require proof! Page 68

LET ME HEAR FROM YOU!

I want to know if the concept of spiritual danger areas and this process for dealing with them is helpful to you. I also would appreciate any ideas you have had for better recognition of spiritual danger areas in the world of work and protocols that you have found to work (croushornjim@AOL.com).

It is my prayer that you will get prepared and stay alert in your jungle.

Welcome to the Jungle

THOUSANDS OF CHRISTIAN young people graduate from high school and college every year and enter the world of work. Many have had years of Bible study and discipleship. I fear that many still remain unprepared for the spiritual danger areas they will encounter in the workplace. They need some intensive jungle training before they enter this new environment.

I challenge all churches to have a "Welcome to the Jungle" weekend retreat for their young people each spring before graduation, to introduce them to the idea of spiritual danger areas in the workplace. Every church has many Spiritual Warriors who have successfully lived their faith in the world of work. Have them get together and format their experience in terms of spiritual danger areas, and protocols that have worked for them.

Then have a panel make a presentation, followed by questions from the young people. The discussion that would follow should provide an understanding of spiritual danger areas, alerts that can trigger their awareness that a danger area is there, and protocols that have worked for the Christian men and women on the panel. This would be one additional tool that could help young Christians who will soon be entering this new spiritual environment.

Are You a Christian?

I CAN'T UNDERSTAND why you have picked up this book if you are not a Christian. But for some reason you have, and now you find yourself reading this section. Listen, what a Christian is and how to become one is somewhat complicated and difficult to understand without faith. Faith is what makes all of this work.

I am not a preacher or a minister. I want to explain this to you in down to earth, everyday terms, in my own words. I am intentionally going to be very direct and confrontational, because I see this as my one and only chance to talk to you.

My urgency in this presentation comes from my concern for you to consider what I believe is the absolutely most important thing you have ever thought about. If my presentation results in helping you "find God," you will find, as have millions through the ages, that your life will never be the same.

First of all, I think you have to finally come to the conclusion that there is something more to your life, to you, than skin and bones and blood and all of those things that make you an animal. That "something" is what you are without that body. It's your person. You've probably seen a dead body at some time in your life. As an adult you have been to a funeral or visitation at the funeral home. If so, you have probably looked at that body and realized that what that person was has gone. It is not in that body any more.

Among those things that are no longer a part of that body is what we Christians believe to be the soul. We believe that the soul continues to live beyond the death of that body. We have no proof of this, but based on the teachings of the Bible, we accept on faith that is true. If you don't believe there is something about you that goes beyond your body, then you will have a difficult time understanding the rest of what I have to say about the definition of a Christian, and how you can become one.

You really need to understand how faith works. Faith does not require proof. In fact, proof negates faith. If you have proof you do not need faith. Have you ever just come in the house and sat down in a chair? Did you first go through the process of asking whether or not that chair would hold you when you sat in it? Did you look at the design of the chair and analyze the construction before you released all of your weight on that chair? Probably not! You accepted on faith that the chair would do its job. **FAITH DOES NOT REQUIRE PROOF!**

There has to be more to life than bodily functions and human survival. Let's say that, on faith, you accept the idea that you have a soul and that it lives after your body dies. If this soul exists, why? What purpose does the soul serve? We

Christians accept that each human being has a soul and that there is a purpose for that soul's existence. To accept this will be your first step of faith.

The next step has to do with an awareness that there is a higher being, a being that is all-powerful and all knowing. We Christians call this being God. Now there is a need to connect this notion that you have a soul with the notion that there is a higher being. What is that connection?

Read the early chapters of Genesis and you will see that the original purpose of man's creation was to satisfy God's need for companionship. God has needs, you ask? Yes, God has needs, and one of his biggest original needs was for companionship. The early chapters of Genesis tell this story. I like the way the poet, James Weldon Johnson, describes the creation of man in his poem "The Creation." It begins with the following verse:

> And God stepped out on space,
> And he looked around and said:
> I'm lonely—
> I'll make me a world.[1]

Man was made not only with a capacity for a relationship with his creator, but also with a programmed need for that relationship. As someone has described it, man was made with a God shaped space inside his soul that can only be filled by God. The Bible says that man was made in God's image.

Any interest or desire that you are experiencing now that brings you to this appendix is the desire to fill that emptiness, and to fill it with God. You may be experiencing an awareness that something is missing in your life. There is something that you cannot satisfy no matter how you try.

We Christians believe that what is missing is a personal relationship with God.

The Bible is very plain that it was God's intent that man would always be in a real and healthy relationship with his creator. But God gave man a free will. He did not make us robots, automatons, or clones. He wanted a relationship with a creature that could make choices about his life, including his relationship with his creator.

You know the story. Man chose worldly pleasures (the eating of that forbidden fruit) over his relationship with God. The consequence was a break in man's relationship with God and his expulsion from the Garden of Eden. Note in your reading of Genesis that it was man who walked away from God. God has always been there wanting and inviting man back into that original relationship. The rest of the Old Testament tells the story of God's progressive revelation of himself to man. The New Testament tells the story of God's ultimate revelation of himself, Jesus.

Let me throw in something here that many non-Christians as well as Christians stumble over. That is the theory of evolution vs. creationism. For me this "controversy" is not important to my personal relationship with God. There is nothing in the process of coming to a "personal relationship" with God that requires you to accept one or the other theory. These are only theories because no one living today was actually there. The critical element in this controversy is for you to believe that all of creation came from God. Whether he did it in seven 24 hour periods, or over eons of time through seven geological periods, is not important to your coming into a personal relationship with God. Don't let unanswered questions in your mind stop you from finding and experiencing a personal relationship with God.

Christians believe that God's ultimate revelation to man was in Jesus Christ. God became man so that man could know God. How simple! Jesus was in a pure relationship with God because he is God. Is that confusing to you? It is somewhat to me. But I accept that "God the Father" has an element that Christians refer to as "God the Son." Now that is Jesus.

There is also "God the Holy Spirit." That is the element of God that comes into your being when you accept all of this on faith. I once heard a story about the American Indian's idea of conscience. It was described as a box that turns when you do something wrong. When it turns, the corners of the box hurt you inside. The more it turns as a result of our doing and thinking wrong, the corners wear down until it turns and we barely feel it. The entry of the Holy Spirit into your life when you become a Christian is like getting a new box. If it has really happened then you will experience an awareness of a Presence in your life.

The second purpose for Jesus was to be THE way by which all men could once again have a personal relationship with God, just like the one that Adam and Eve experienced in the Garden of Eden. That process occurred in the death of Christ on the cross. Christians believe that Christ took on himself the sin of all men for all time. It was the supreme gift of God that by accepting the death and resurrection of Jesus, and asking for forgiveness for his own sins, man could enter into a personal relationship with Christ.

To the non-Christian, I know this sounds strange. But it is true that this simple act can transform your life into one where God as the Holy Spirit enters your soul and establishes a real personal relationship with you. This is stated in John 3:16, "For God so loved the world that he gave his only begotten Son that whosoever believes in him shall have everlasting life." If you accept that verse on faith, ... you are a Christian!

Becoming a Christian may or may not be an emotional experience for you. Most people have about as much emotion in their religious experience as they have in the rest of their life. But the key to this transformation is FAITH that it is true and has occurred. Experiencing God comes after your "conversion," after you have accepted God into your life on faith. Think of it in human turns. You meet a new person; perhaps someone with whom you fall in love. If that has ever happened, you know that every moment thereafter that person is a part of all that you think and do, even when you are not in that person's physical presence. Getting to know God is kind of like that. It is after you have "ACCEPTED HIM INTO YOUR LIFE" that a change in your attitude, thinking, and peace of mind occurs, and you become aware that the emptiness inside you is finally filled.

If you are not at the point of committing to this personal relationship in faith yet, let me ask you to read the New Testament Book of John. Read it three or four times and let it really sink into your heart and mind. See if that doesn't help you understand who and what Jesus is, and what faith does to make all of this work.

Becoming a Christian is hard to understand, but easy to do! So "just do it"!

If you are now a Christian return to $\boxed{\text{X}}$ on page 16 of the text.

How to Remove All Doubt About Your Conversion

AFTER I BECAME a Christian I prayed many times that God would reveal himself to me in some real, physical, undeniable way so that I would be propelled into a dynamic ministry based on a dynamic revelation of God. I prayed that prayer because many times I doubted my conversion experience. I wanted a "Damascus Road experience," just like the apostle Paul.

I became a Christian when I was nine years old, during Vacation Bible School at the First Baptist Church in Birmingham, Alabama, in 1948. I recall being very aware that God had "saved" me, and understanding the meaning of baptism and joining the church. I grew up as a "goody-goody" kid, largely thanks to my mom who was the daughter of a Baptist preacher. Her father was Joseph Edward Lowry, pastor of 12th Street Baptist Church in Gadsden, Alabama, in the 1920's.

During my childhood, Mom made sure I went to Sunday school and church. All of this led to my growing up without a lot of "sinful" behavior. For example, I never persecuted any Christians like Paul. It was in my thinking that some of Paul's reaction to his "Damascus Road Experience" had to be related to the very bad life he led before his conversion. The difference in his behavior after his conversion was dynamic, undeniable, as clearly different as night is from day. Oh how I wanted that kind of a real encounter with God. It was my constant prayer, often when I was alone and at night.

One of my duties as the part time music and youth director for my home church, Birmingham's Ninth Avenue Baptist Church, was to do the Sunday morning bulletin. In those days before computers, 1958 - 1962, the way you did the bulletin was to type the words on a stencil, put the stencil on the mimeograph machine, and run the bulletin paper through the machine. Being a young, single college student, who was very much interested in finding one of those Howard College girls to marry, it was not unusual for me to go by the church after my Saturday night date to do the bulletins. It was often midnight or later before I got around to doing that task.

Ninth Avenue was a church in an old but adequate building for our congregation, with an attendance of about 200 in Sunday School each Sunday. The only door that had an outside lock was the front door of the sanctuary. However, the light switch for the sanctuary lights was back by the baptismal pool behind the pulpit. The church office was behind the sanctuary in the "educational wing." So...after finishing the bulletin, I would have to turn the lights off and walk through the dark sanctuary to the front door, so I could lock the door to the church as I left.

Early one Sunday morning, about 1:00 AM, having completed the bulletin, I was ready to leave the church. I turned out the lights and entered the sanctuary. As I often did, I was praying that God would reveal himself to me in some physical and undeniable way. Just after I prayed that prayer and turned in front of the church to walk down the center aisle, my hand brushed something "physical and undeniable" right there in the middle of the aisle at the front of the church. I swung around and knelt down, convinced that God had appeared in response to my prayer. As I knelt there, speaking to God, my eyes gradually adjusted to the dark. I began to see that it wasn't God that I had touched, but rather a lectern that someone had left in the middle of the aisle. Relieved that I had not had a heart attack when I had believed I was face-to-face with God, but disappointed that my longed for "real, dynamic, physical encounter with God" had not occurred, I stood up and proceeded through the dark sanctuary.

I believe that honesty must come with conversion, particularly being honest with yourself. Although I had been a Christian for quite some time, I still did not understand the dynamics of faith when it came to my conversion, because truthfully there were times I didn't feel saved.

While living a Christian life the best I knew how, I continued to pray for a "Damascus Road experience." This desire lasted throughout college, and after graduation, as I began working for the welfare department in Birmingham, while serving part time as the music and youth director at the First Baptist Church in Ashland, Alabama. A year later, as I entered the Army, I was still praying for that undeniable encounter with God.

In Korea in 1965-66, there was a shortage of chaplains because at that time virtually everything was going to Vietnam. Missionaries were our chaplains. A Navigator missionary was assigned to my unit, the 1st Brigade of the 2nd Infantry Division. I got involved in their Bible studies. I learned a lot from the Navigators, but continued to desire that "real encounter with God."

When I returned to the states I was stationed at Ft. Benning in Columbus Georgia. I was assigned as the Custodian of the Youth Activities Club. All of the dependent children's activities came under my shop.

I moved into the Navigator home in Columbus. I became very active in the Navigator Ministry (http://www.gospelcom.net/navs/), including participating in the Bible Studies. I remember one Bible study that was about the relationship of the disciples to Jesus. During the study, I had commented that I found it very interesting that Judas had the same encounter with Jesus as the other disciples, but "it had not taken." The contact Judas had was real, but it had not changed his life.

After the Bible study one of the Navs came up to me and complemented me on a very meaningful insight. I then told him that I still struggled with a desire to have a "real undeniable encounter with God," a "Damascus Road" encounter like Paul. I told him that I felt that such an experience would remove the doubt I sometimes had that my conversion was not real. I wanted an encounter that would erase all my doubt and compel me never to question my salvation again.

My Navigator friend suggested that in order to remove that doubt I should pray the "sinners prayer." I was to pray that God would forgive me of my sins and enter my heart (Romans 10:9). After I prayed that prayer I should then observe my life objectively. If there was no change in my life, then I should accept on faith that my conversion had been genuine and that my relationship with God was real.

I prayed that prayer. There was no change in my behavior, thinking, or spiritual experience. I concluded that my original conversion was real. I was a Christian with a real relationship with God. I accepted that on faith. Since then I have never prayed that prayer for a Damascus Road experience. Since then there has never been a single instance of self-doubt of my conversion.

I recommend this process to you. If you have ever questioned your salvation, and desired a "Damascus Road experience" like Paul's to validate your conversion, I challenge you to pray the "sinners prayer" on faith. You will either confirm your previous experience, or you will have a real encounter with God. The bottom line = no more doubts regarding your conversion.

If you are now a "confident" Christian, return to $\boxed{\text{Y}}$ on page 16 of the text.

The Serious Spiritual Warrior

By SERIOUS I MEAN a person who is not "playing" with his religion like a hobby.

Do you remember when, as a teenager, you had a part time job in a fast food restaurant or delivering pizza? You wanted to do a good job. You were serious enough to show up for work and do the best you could for your boss. But the consequences of all you did were minor.

The "serious" that I am talking about is having a serious job. A job that has important consequences. Your performance at work, both good and bad, has serious consequences. There are implications for your future career, the economic well being of your family and your work organization. So you take your actions seriously.

Serious also involves focus and concentration. The task at hand has your full attention. The wide receiver in football knows what he has to do to run the prescribed pattern of the play that has been called. He goes out and concentrates and focuses on the pattern he must run without being distracted by the defensive back. He does this no matter how many times he has done this before and been knocked down. He does this knowing that he will probably get knocked down and hammered again. But he knows if he can hold his focus and execute, he will be where he is supposed to be when the quarterback throws the ball. Now that is concentration and focus.

The serious Christian should have this kind of concentration and focus on living up to his relationship with God every hour of every day.

Now apply all of that to living your faith. Are you focused on the impact of your faith on others? Are you aware of the impact of what you do as a Christian or of what you do not do? Do you care about the consequences of living your faith? If not, you are not taking your personal relationship with God seriously. Grow Up! Living your faith in the workplace is not a game. It is deadly serious with eternal consequences. Being fully aware and focusing on living your faith 24/7 as if in a hostile jungle is a requirement of the Spiritual Warrior.

If you are there, then return to $\boxed{Z}$ on page 17 of the text and learn about spiritual danger areas and tools for victorious Christian living in the world of work.

Worksheet:

Identifying and Responding to a Spiritual Danger Area on the Job

Description of a spiritual challenge you face on the job.

_____

_____

_____

_____

_____

ALERT TRIGGER Describe the thought, event, person, or situation that makes you first aware that the spiritual challenge is upon you.

_____

_____

Describe Actions You Can Take to Avoid the Spiritual Challenge.

Develop the Protocol. Describe Actions You Can Take to Successfully Overcome the Spiritual Challenge When It Can Not Be Avoided.

ENDNOTES

Introduction

[1] Name changed in order to be sensitive to the pain and grief of the family.

[2] S. L. A. Marshall, *Battles in the Monsoons,*

[3] Note: I'm the one on the third row from the top, sixth man from the left at the Internet site:

http://www.benning.army.mil/rtb/ranger/photo/1-66.ipg.

For more on the U.S. Army Ranger School go to:

http://207.234.171.162/rangers/rangers.htm

[4] Ephesians 6: 12

Chapter 1

[1] Frank Peretti, *This Present Darkness*, Crossway Books, August 1989.

[2] Ephesians 6: 12

[3] Barber, Brace E., *Ranger School: No Excuse Leadership*, Patrol Leader Press, 1999.

Chapter 2

[1] Ranger Handbook, SH21-76, July 1992, Chapter 4-5;

[2] Ranger Handbook, Page 4-19, paragraph 4-5 a.

[3] Thanks to Dr. Gene Sherron for the wording of this paragraph.

[4] Ranger Handbook, Pages 6-18 & 19, paragraph 9.b.

Chapter 3

[1] New International Version

[2] Ephesians 6: 10-18a

[3] Ephesians 6: 18b

[4] Romans 7: 14a-20

[5] Acts 9: 3

Chapter 5

[1] 2 Samuel 11:2-3

[2] I thank Ellen Williams, one of the people I interviewed, for this excellent analogy.

[3] Encyclopedia Britannica, Vol 9, p. 112.

Appendix A

[1] James Weldon Johnson, *God's Trombones: Seven Negro Sermons in Verse*, Viking Press, 1927, p. 17.

About the Author

"THE FIRST TIME I ever thought of administration as a life's work was in 1968 in a discussion with Dr. Ruth Schafer, my faculty advisor at the University of Alabama Graduate School of Social Work. I told her that I thought the most idealistic way to spend my life would be to get a doctorate in Social Work and return to the welfare department in Birmingham and do good things with my 50 cases of Aid to Dependent Children. Dr. Schaffer replied, 'Croushorn you are wrong. Idealism is not always best expressed at the point of confrontation. If you can do good things with 50 cases, you can do more as a supervisor of five case workers which would influence what happens with 250 cases.' From that day forward I focused on becoming an administrator."

After graduating from Samford University in 1962 and serving three years of active duty in the U.S. Army, Jim received his Masters in Social Work from the University of Alabama (1970) as well as a Masters in Public Administration (1971). Three years in Athens, Georgia resulted in a

Doctor of Public Administration (1974). This was followed by four years teaching Social Welfare Administration at the University of Tennessee Graduate School of Social Work.

Since 1978 Jim has worked in various administrative positions in the Florida Department of Health and Rehabilitative Services and the Florida Department of Health. Currently he is the Administrative Officer for Emergency Operations, Florida Department of Health.

Of the gifts of the Holy Spirit described in 1 Corinthians 12, Jim most closely identifies with the gift of administration (12:28). "I believe that we are all called to ministry. Every Christian should approach the way he earns his living as a call of God. I truly believe that God has called me into government as an administrator."

Jim is married to Linda Barron Croushorn, an elementary school assistant principal in Tallahassee. He and Linda have two children. Their son John is an M.D. who lives in Jackson, Mississippi with his wife Julie and their two children, Caleb and Katie. Their daughter, Amy Lynn, is an interior designer in Atlanta.

The author, Jim Croushorn